AN ANTHOLOGY OF THE WITNESSED

SUBHO MUKHOPADHYAY

Made with ♥ on the Notion Press Platform
www.notionpress.com

To my dear little Stella who lights up my entire world and to my dogs, my boys Simba and Salva who have shown me the true sense of unconditional love

Contents

Preface

The moment we start perceiving the different wavelengths around us, that is when the stories reach our ears - the tales of sorrow, fear, and ecstasy. We let them reciprocate themselves in their most direct forms, we do not ask why, where, who, when or how. We listen, we share and we grow and become the harbingers of life. Evolution is slow but it is inevitable and we take everything along with us - be it the good or bad, we make them a part of ourselves.

Acknowledgements

I would like to take a moment to thank a few friends of mine who have always been an inspiration to me from the very first day when I started writing - maybe one of the reasons why I see myself being a poet years from now.

1. The big day

Leftovers from the rich's plates,
To the cold and shivering could be the first grains.
Do the lights bring a smile to the dispossessed?
Elation? Or do the carols bring solace instead?
To those for whom each day is a brawl
And even a thread of linen has the earmarks of a Pashmina Shawl!
Dear Lord as they pray,
With dust on their hands they mumble the words away.
Inflicted upon by the worst of nature,
Every day they wake pinning their hopes on God for something better!
When do we unite, is it when we notice or when we act?
Isn't there a little space for all those?
Isn't there a little share of bread?
Turning our eyes away is not what they deserve to get!

2. Friday the 15th

The sounds of the gunfire,
Running through sleepless nights,
As the tremors of revolt started
Marching towards a relentless fight.
With heads held high,
With hands like steel,
With the spines made of resolve
Out they came with a zeal!
A tyrant on the loose,
Reigning lands of others,
A nation at stake
Uniting all the sisters and brothers.
All the sacrifices made,
The dreams of free land,
Seen together-
Came true fighting hand in hand.

3. The west sky

A closure,
From things unrestrained,
A fading light at the
Road's end.
The song of nothingness,
Flying amidst a broken world,
A failed attempt-
At making things unfurl!

4. In love we do trust

Something I love,
When the skies are above,
When the earth smells fresh
From the first rain.
That takes away all the pain-
From within us,
In love we do trust!
Something I love,
When the mountains smile,
When the trees play
With the birds today,
A mischievous game
It takes away all the pain-
From within us,
In love we do trust!
Something I love,
When the rivers sing,
To the tunes of the rocks,
They paint a story together every day
And it takes away,
All the pain
From within us,
In love we do trust!

5. A dream for a better world

When hope leaves a sigh,
In the face of time,
The truth sets in
With the waters running high.
The leaves no longer sing
To the breezy tunes on the street,
The lonely dog looks for
Pieces of litter to eat!
Humanity falls and sufferings rise-
The sun shines no longer with pride.
The nuances of those in power
Are revealed to the human eyes,
What the world witnesses
Is the saddest story in plain sight!

6. The riddle

Like the far flowing gentle breeze,
You kiss me as you go,
I am the boat tossed in the river of love,
What is true, how do I know!
I am a scientist,
You are the time I am trying to hold,
You are the light I am trying to seize-
You leave with conundrums to unfold!

7. The unwinnable

You are like those waves,
That come close, close enough
And then leave-
Every time you break near my feet,
You make me believe,
This time you will stay-
Can I ever touch you?
With tears in my eyes I pray.
So that for few,
More moments we share our presence,
I still see dreams of our coalescence
In love shall we remain,
If we ever meet again!

8. The fib

A colour,
Does it define?
Does it weigh?
Does it have anything else to say?
Than that of another shade,
What does it matter if it's black or white?
My dearest earth mates, why do you fight?
Aren't we all born the same?
Whatever maybe our fame,
Whatever we deserve or get
We all come by red,
We all leave blue.
And yes, that is true!

9. Deoli (dedicated)

When we don't get what we yearn for,
We learn and we earn,
Wisdom and knowledge at one go
And that is how we grow!
It deprives us of joy,
And it leaves us with truth,
Once it gave us hope
Now we remain put!
Dear Mr. Bond,
In a page or two,
You gave us what we are still fond
Of, and you taught us
To move on,
To not be sad yet keep the hopes up
To see dreams, to live in where we are,
To live in what good we had.
And not be sad,
And not be sad,
And not be sad.

10. Turmoil of the three

Are we listening?
To the mindless chorus,
The sounds that rejuvenate
Our senses to the best!
Do we swing along?
To the tunes of where we belong,
Confiding in the lights of laughter-
Time precedes or does it come after?

11. Such goodbyes

Goodbyes are hard,
But still you smile,
When you leave
To embark on distant miles.
The bag by your side,
Laden with love,
With laughter and ecstasy -
You envisage there is a different sky above!
Smells of earth
That had grown inside you,
Still linger on
To days, anew.
The water from the nearby river,
That wet your feet,
Will not dry
Even after you stand on a dry sheet.
You leave but you stay back in parts of you,
Such happenings are very few.
So don't you be sad
Dear traveller - you'll always have a friend,
To come back to,
To whom you'll have the letters to send!

12. The leap of faith

Sometimes you take the leap of faith,
The decisions you make - don't you hate,
It's the bittersweet tune that makes us dance
Till we get to realise when is our chance.
Do we expect or do we hope to win?
Or do we lose and still keep up our chin?
We choose a road and leave the other one behind,
There is no going back once we fixate our mind.
And sometimes we take that leap of faith,
Might we lose or win, our decisions we can never hate!

13. A letter to those who I write for

" It's good that you reached till here,
It's good that you wanted to read,
My words grow because of you my dear
Your support is my creed!
I have come a long way,
I have had my share of right and wrong
Yet a lot more to go,
Till we witness dawn.
I promise to write again
I promise to hear,
The sounds around me
All the stories of love or hate or fear!
We'd venture together
Through every epoch, every era, every eon,
We'll share and we'll care,
We'll go on
I promise to be that good to you the way you have been to me!
Without you, what can I even see?"

9 798889 750505

Printed by Libri Plureos GmbH in Hamburg,
Germany